FEEDBACK
TOOLKIT

FEEDBACK TOOLKIT

---

16 Tools for Better
Communication in the Workplace

Rick Maurer

PRODUCTIVITY PRESS
PORTLAND, OREGON

Productivity Press
P.O. Box 13390
Portland OR 97213-0390
United States of America
Telephone: 503-235-0600
Telefax: 503-235-0909

ISBN: 1-56327-056-0

Cover design by Rohani Design, copyright © by Productivity Press.
Printed and bound by Edwards Brothers in the United States of America

Library of Congress Cataloging-in-Publication Data:

Maurer, Rick
            Feedback toolkit : 16 tools for better communication in the workplace / Rick Maurer.
               p.   cm.
            Includes bibliographical references.
            ISBN 1-56327-056-0 :
            1. Communication in personnel management. 2. Feedback (Psychology) I. Title.
            HF5549.5.C6M29 1994
            658.3'14—dc20   94-11842
                                                                                        CIP

98 97 96 95 94   10 9 8 7 6 5 4 3 2 1

CONTENTS

Publisher's Message vii

Preface xi

■ PART ONE   USING THE TOOLKIT

About Feedback 3

When Feedback Works 7

What Gets in the Way 11

General Guidelines 15

Applying the Guidelines 21

■ PART TWO   TOOLS FOR GIVING FEEDBACK

1 Learning from Mistakes 27

2 A "What Are We Doing?" Meeting 31

3 An Expectations Exchange 35

4 Project Debriefing 39

5 Management by Wandering Around 43
6 Positive Feedback for Teams 47
7 The Performance Appraisal 51
8 Acid Bath Feedback 57

■ PART THREE   TOOLS FOR RECEIVING FEEDBACK

9 Preparing to Receive Feedback 61
10 Guidelines for Receiving Feedback 67
11 Don't Forget SARA 69
12 Feedback from Staff 73
13 Feedback from Your Boss 77
14 Feedback from Peers 81
15 Feedback from a Coach 85
16 Feedback from Questionnaires 89

   Notes 95
   About the Author 97

PUBLISHER'S MESSAGE

Communication is a critical function in the modern workplace. Offices, manufacturing floors, and retail establishments rely increasingly on sophisticated electronic equipment to link employees and give them information they need to perform their jobs. But the information that managers and employees need to share at work is not all found in networks and databases. Especially in companies striving to reduce hierarchy and foster trust and responsible participation, good person-to-person feedback can be as important as computer technology in enabling people to work together effectively.

Many competent managers are understandably uneasy when it comes to giving and receiving this type of information. For some, feedback means saying difficult things to an employee at an annual appraisal meeting. For others, the thought of opening up to potentially critical ideas and perceptions from their employees brings a defensive response.

Rick Maurer's *Feedback Toolkit* addresses this natural hesitation in a simple, straightforward way, beginning Part 1 by defining feedback and telling why effective feedback is important for high performance. Quite simply, feedback is about telling each other the truth—a two-way street between employees and managers. The tools are intended to make it easier to speak the truth in an appropriate way. Feedback gives a map of the situation, a way to tell whether you are "on or off track." "Poor feedback," says Maurer, "leads to performance problems, confusion, wasted effort, anxiety, and work of lower quality."

Maurer, the author of *Caught in the Middle* (Productivity Press, 1992), writes from his experience as an organizational consultant, helping people in a wide range of settings change the way they work together; the methods in the *Toolkit* have been used successfully by managers in a variety of situations. The better managers, Maurer finds, are generally those who are better at giving and receiving feedback. In Part 1 he summarizes the approaches these great managers use, as well as some of the organizational obstacles to good feedback. He sets out a number of guidelines, then condenses them into an easy-to-grasp 6-step framework that becomes the structure for each of the tools later presented.

Parts 2 and 3 of the book offer an array of creative but practical approaches to use for various situations. Part 2 focuses on tools for giving feedback. Some are for one-on-one dialogues, others are frameworks for group discussions. Maurer, who agrees with the late Dr. Deming on the questionable value of annual performance reviews, nevertheless offers suggestions for coping with the process, as well as for giving unpleasant work-related feedback.

The tools in Part 3 offer guidance in receiving feedback from various sources—one's peers, boss, staff members, customers. Recognizing that it can be difficult to hear from others how you can be more effective, Maurer begins with exercises on getting ready to take this leap; his discussion of "SARA" will be very helpful in coming to terms with the range of emotions that can come up.

We are pleased to work with Rick Maurer on this book and expect that readers will find it a practical and useful companion to *Caught in the Middle.* Thanks as well to Jodi Sleeper-Triplett of Maurer & Associates for her assistance. A number of other people helped bring out this book; our thanks go to: Bob Shoemaker, president of Productivity Press; Diane Asay, acquisitions editor; Karen Jones, managing editor; Bill Stanton, production manager; Susan Swanson, production coordinator; Rohani Design, cover and interior design and composition.

Norman Bodek
Publisher

PREFACE

As a result of the publication of my book, *Caught in the Middle: A Leadership Guide for Partnership in the Workplace* (Productivity Press, 1992), I learned that people were hungry for tools that could assist them in working with others more effectively. Although I listed many tips and suggestions in the book, people seemed to want even more ideas—especially on feedback.

This handbook is a compilation of ideas that others have shared with me; approaches I developed as a coordinator of the feedback process in the Leadership development Program (a Center for Creative Leadership program) at the University of Maryland; and tools that I have used successfully with my consulting clients.

ACKNOWLEDGMENTS

I sent the first draft of *Feedback Toolkit* to a number of managers and asked them to use the tools they found useful and valuable. I include some of their comments verbatim in the text. My thanks to Mark Ackelson, Mary Brooks, Douglas DeVries, Margo Freeberg, JoAn Knight Herren, Joe Hill, Richard Hornaday, Gerald Lyner, Sheree Parris Nudd, Leigh Reid, Frank Rodgers, Ruth Voor, and Pat Whelan. (Since I started this project quite a while ago, I imagine I have forgotten others who gave helpful advice. I apologize for any omissions.)

A special thanks to the following for giving me permission to use tools that they either developed or refined: Ellen Harvey for the "'What Are We Doing?' Meeting"; Caela Farren, Beverly Kaye, and Zandy Leibowitz for the "Expectations Exchange" and Mike Korgie for the manager/staff variation; and David Coleman for "Positive Feedback for Teams."

— Rick Maurer

PART ONE

USING THE TOOLKIT

"ALWAYS TELL THE TRUTH, IT'S THE EASIEST THING TO REMEMBER."

— DAVID MAMET

ABOUT
FEEDBACK

In this book, I offer tools to make it easier for people to tell each other the truth. These tools provide structures—rituals, if you will—that can make it safer for you and your colleagues to engage in honest dialogue.

The tools are like maps—they point the way, warn you about potential trouble spots, and give you a picture of the terrain—but they can't drive the car for you. That's your job. Some trips are easy, scenic, and memorable. Others are like a *National Lampoon Vacation*, where everything seems to go wrong.

The better you know the terrain under various driving conditions, the easier it will be for you to antici-pate hazards, estimate time, and drive safely.

Feedback is information that lets us know whether we are on or off track. So simple, and yet so difficult.

According to surveys in *Fortune* and *Industry Week*,[1] most people in organizations don't get sufficient feedback. The lower you go in an organization, the less feedback is given; the higher you go, the better people think they are doing at giving it. In other words, we believe we do a better job at giving feedback than we really do.

Poor feedback leads to performance problems, confusion, wasted effort, anxiety, and work of lower quality. I consulted to an organization in which an entire division was confused about how it fit into the company's strategic direction. People didn't know whether they were on target or off, and they found it difficult to get answers to their questions. As a result, when they were in doubt, they simply invented their own performance criteria.

Effective feedback can do many things:

- Feedback honors competence and reinforces behavior you are looking for.

- Feedback helps align expectations and priorities.

- Feedback fills gaps in knowledge.

- Feedback lets people know where to take corrective action.

- Feedback alleviates fear of the unknown.

The handbook is written for you. The *Feedback Toolkit* includes many simple tools you can use to improve feedback in your work unit. The tools are informal, and are meant to be adapted to your particular circumstances. Most of them will work just as well whether you are in a paneled corporate office or leaning against a piece of heavy equipment on a shop floor.

When
Feedback Works

As I prepared to write *Caught in the Middle: A Leadership Guide for Partnership in the Workplace*, I began to note many things that distinguish managers who have good working relationships with staff from those who are less successful. Not surprisingly, the better managers are generally better at giving and receiving feedback.

Here are a few communication approaches that set the best managers apart:

They just do it. These managers don't wait to become perfect at giving feedback. They know it is important and they just haul off and give it. Sometimes they do it inelegantly, but they earn-while-they-learn and get better with practice.

They give feedback frequently and informally. They don't wait for performance appraisal time—they find many opportunities to give people the information they need.

They focus on the customer. They direct feedback toward making things better for an external customer—or for the folks down the hall. This approach keeps the conversation focused on what is truly important and away from personal opinions. These managers know they are in business to serve customers/clients/users/the public, and they give feedback with that purpose in mind.

They seek feedback. The best managers find ways to get feedback from their staff. This is a bit surprising, since most organizational structures emphasize top-down feedback and offer no formal way for a boss to receive it. These people have to *work* at getting the feedback they need.

They find ways to get around the system. Some organizations create extraordinary mazes through which feedback is supposed to flow. When the formal system doesn't work or creates hassles, these managers take a chance and go around the system.

They build a foundation. These managers realize that the higher the trust level within the office, the easier it is for people to give and receive feedback. They create ways for people to get to know one another, so that feedback sessions aren't meetings between strangers.

WHAT GETS
IN THE WAY

As important as it is to realize what works, we must also realize what doesn't work and recognize the ways in which we limit our own effectiveness.

Here are some aspects of management that hinder effective communication of feedback.

Feedback is top-down. In the traditional organizational model, feedback travels only downhill. Even though most performance review systems reinforce this faulty approach, it is critically important to tell the emperor when he or she has forgotten to dress in the morning.

It is not rewarded. You no doubt have heard that what gets rewarded gets done. If giving feedback is viewed as

11

"nice" to do, but not essential, people usually will not engage in it.

Management by exception. We are all busy, and as a result we may give feedback only when something goes wrong. This allows problems to build to a breaking point—and conversely, it makes it too easy to forget to say "thank you" for the little things.

Performance appraisal system. Performance review is the worst time to give feedback to an employee. You are nervous and the recipient is taking an acid bath. These conditions are not conducive to a productive conversation about performance.

Fear. Fear is a major motivator. We are afraid we might hurt their feelings, or that they might lash out at us. We fear that we don't have all the facts. It doesn't take much fear to give us grand rationalizations for not giving someone feedback at the appropriate time.

I hope that this handbook will help you overcome some of these obstacles—even fear. If you use these tools to give and receive feedback frequently, things won't have a chance to build up. You can begin using feedback as a daily management tool—rather than saving up information to pass on during a dreaded annual performance review. But remember, these tools offer no easy answer.

For most of us, giving and receiving feedback is extremely difficult. Respect that. Don't take on more than you or your colleagues can handle.

GENERAL
GUIDELINES

Here a few things to keep in mind any time you are preparing to give feedback:

Identify the business reason. Most feedback should be directed toward meeting some business-related goal—for example, to improve the service your unit provides to customers, or to increase efficiency of product delivery.

Ask yourself, Why is it important to give this person feedback? If you can't identify a solid business reason, you may be giving feedback for the wrong reasons. You may at times want to give feedback just to clear the air—to get something off your chest. I recommend that you not give feedback under those circumstances.

Focus on the future. Too often feedback gets mired in past transgressions. That makes the recipient feel bad—and defensive. The past is over. You want performance to improve *in the future*. Give sufficient data about past performance so that the person understands your concern, then discuss how things could be different *in the future*.

Use customer data. When possible, use internal or external customer data as the basis for your feedback. If your organization focuses on meeting customer expectations (and it should), then your feedback helps address this critical challenge. Customer-oriented feedback is far better than feedback that is limited to your opinion of what is good and bad.

Put it in context. Is this a big issue or a minor problem? A major achievement or small win? If we launch into the feedback without saying how important it is, the other person's attention is directed on figuring out the severity of the discussion rather than on listening to you.

> 💬 Chris, I need to talk with you about project status reports. I want you to know that this isn't a major problem. In fact, I see this discussion as simply fine-tuning. 💬

Be specific. Give people tangible examples of the performance you want them to change or continue.

“ The status reports are usually three to five days late and are often incomplete with regard to expenditures. Let's look at last week's report. From now on, I would like to get the report on Friday, and I'll need complete budget breakout in these categories. **”**

Make it timely. If feedback is going to help, it needs to be given near the time of the event. If you wait for months, people may wonder just how important the issue is to you. Timely feedback also ensures that people remember the event. It is hard to discuss something when the other person doesn't recall the details.

Find someplace private. When feedback is negative, people need to be able to save face. Public hangings may feel good to you, but may severely hurt the individual involved. Beyond the stuckee's reaction, your public display sends a powerful message to the entire staff about your leadership style.

Find someplace public. Although some people are embarrassed by public praise (and you should honor this reticence), most often you should criticize in private, praise in public. Most people like to hear they did well. Public praise also lets others know that you appreciate good work.

Keep it simple and slow. If you have a lot of negative things to say, consider focusing just on the most important concerns. People can take in only so much before they are overwhelmed. If the feedback is detailed, slow down. Give people a chance to take in the information, swallow it, and digest it. Even though you may be nervous and want to get the encounter over with, you increase your chances of being heard if you move slowly.

Focus on behavior, not individuals. You are trying to improve or reinforce work performance. Stick with the behavior and avoid personalities. Statements such as "People like you always..." are needlessly inflammatory.

Explain the impact. Be sure to tell the recipient the impact the behavior is having on you, on the organization, and on the customer. Let the person know why the issue is important.

> ❝ Mary, your delay in getting these chapters to me slows down the entire project. I get behind. My boss keeps asking for my comments on the work, and the editor is forced to work overtime to try to stay close to schedule. ❞

Speak from the heart. The business world is rational. Our meetings are littered with "I think" statements. This language of the head dominates most exchanges at work, and it often serves us well. However, when we have been hurt or betrayed, feel manipulated, or become cautious, this language fails to communicate. We must state our feelings and articulate the pain.

> **"** Pat, when you promised Sales that we could deliver everything next week, I felt as if you had no respect for me. I've explained repeatedly that those promises just make me look bad with the others whose work is going to be slowed down. **"**

Speak for yourself. Don't act as if you are the spokesperson for the ambiguous *them*. "They aren't too pleased with..." Speak in the first person. Explain how *you* think and feel. Tell the person the impact his/her actions have on you.

Be spontaneous. If you feel an issue should be discussed, you are probably right. Don't wait, do it now. The only exception: if you are angry, wait until your blood pressure drops below 250 to proceed.

Don't inflict feedback. People can take in just so much at one time. Once you exceed what others can handle, they will try to protect themselves from harm. In these situations, you risk never meeting your goals. (See "SARA" in Part Two.)

Feedback is much more than just sharing performance information. Feedback can build a relationship between you and your staff in which you can learn to count on each other. Having the courage to tell the truth and ask for it in return increases trust and our ability to work together.

APPLYING
THE GUIDELINES

The guidelines described on the preceding pages may seem a bit unwieldy. "OK, I've got to remember to be specific, explain the impact, speak from the heart, be sure to listen, put it in context..."

As a reluctant gunfighter in *The Paleface*, Bob Hope is forced into a duel at high noon. As he walks down the street, people rush from all sides to offer advice. "He's left-handed, so lean to your right." "He's very tall, so crouch down." "He's very quick, so keep your hand on your gun." As more and more well-wishers give him helpful tips, Hope's walk becomes cluttered with techniques, and his ability to act is increasingly impaired. You may be feeling the same.

Review the guidelines, then don't worry about them—you'll have enough to think about. After the feedback exchange, review the guidelines once again as a way of critiquing what works for you and what can be improved next time.

Here is a simple way to integrate most of the guidelines. I will use this step structure to describe all the tools in this book.

- **PREPARE**
  Consider the business reason to receive feedback
  Determine the best time and place
  Get the information you need
  Determine how to support yourself

- **PRESENT**
  Give the business reason
  Offer specific examples
  Explain the impact on the organization and on you personally

- **LISTEN**
  Hear the other person's point of view
  Listen with open ears

- **ENGAGE IN DIALOGUE**
  Hold a conversation
  Listen to each other

- **PLAN FOR ACTION**
  Search for solutions that all can agree to

- **ACKNOWLEDGE**
  Thank the person and acknowledge what you have accomplished together

PART TWO

TOOLS FOR

GIVING FEEDBACK

" GOOD JUDGMENT COMES FROM EXPERIENCE. EXPERIENCE COMES FROM MAKING BAD JUDGMENTS. **"**

— MARK TWAIN

LEARNING
FROM MISTAKES

(FOR INDIVIDUALS OR TEAMS)

Mistakes are learning opportunities. Quality improvement gurus such as the late W. Edwards Deming have suggested that over 85% of all performance problems are systems problems. The individual or the team may not be at fault, but something in the overall process makes it difficult to succeed. Perhaps management is giving conflicting messages about priorities, or the computer system breaks down at crucial times.

Consider discussing major breakdowns not as failures, but as *learning opportunities*. The following steps, though directed at providing individual feedback, are equally effective in working with teams.

PREPARE

Before the meeting with the individual or the team, make sure you have a clear picture of what the problem is. These steps are described for a one-on-one meeting but can be adapted for brainstorming with a team.

PRESENT

Tell him/her that you want to discuss an important business issue—not to find blame, but to see what both of you can learn from this experience.

Ask if he/she believes that the issue is worthy of discussion.

LISTEN

Ask for his/her opinion of what broke down.

- Listen carefully.

- Ask questions that help you understand his/her point of view.

- Don't agree or disagree; just be curious and gather information.

ENGAGE IN DIALOGUE

Give your opinion as to what broke down. Talk about the issue.

PLAN FOR ACTION

Identify what both of you can do in the future to minimize the chance that this learning opportunity will turn into a failure.

ACKNOWLEDGE

Thank him/her for taking part in this discussion.

VARIATION

Scott Markey, a district claims manager with Progressive Casualty Insurance, advertises his own mistakes to his staff. By discussing mistakes as *learning opportunities,* he not only learns ways to improve, but also lets others see that it is better to discuss *failures* than to ignore them.

If you want to apply Scott's idea, use your own learning opportunity as the issue and follow the steps listed above.

PAY ATTENTION TO

For group brainstorming, it is important to give people time to think about the issues involved before holding a meeting.

We are not used to discussing mistakes with others. Expect people to be reluctant—they may wonder what you are going to do with the information. Will it appear on a performance review? Your first discussion may yield little, but be grateful for what you get, and keep at it.

Once people realize that you are serious—and that their honesty will not come back to haunt them—they will participate more openly in these discussions.

A "WHAT ARE WE DOING?" MEETING

(FOR TEAMS OR WORK GROUPS)

Philip Crosby talks about *dehassling* the work environment. Here is a very simple technique that might give you a surprising amount of information about the petty hassles that get in the way of high-quality work.

PREPARE

No preparation is needed other than making sure you have a room and flip chart or white board to write down responses.

PRESENT

Ask the group to think about the hassles of their daily activities. Then ask, What are we doing now that we might be able to *stop* doing?

LISTEN

Everyone—including you—brainstorms ideas. Record the responses on flip chart or board.

- Remember that during the brainstorming, responses are recorded without discussion.

- Allow silence. Often people come up with a few ideas and then need time to think. Don't assume silence means that people are finished.

ENGAGE IN DIALOGUE

Sort the responses. It is likely that each suggestion will fall into one of three categories:

- *A keeper.* Everyone agrees that this activity can be stopped with no negative consequence.

- *One for consideration.* You may question whether an internal or external customer really needs this activity anymore.

- *Just a dream.* It would be wonderful if you could be rid of this activity, but you recognize that you are doomed to repeat it for all eternity.

PLAN FOR ACTION

Clarify (so that everyone understands and agrees) which activities will be eliminated as a result of the meeting.

Determine actions the group will take to explore whether some of the "ones for consideration" can be eliminated.

ACKNOWLEDGE
Thank everyone for taking part.

VARIATION
Consider holding these meetings quarterly. They will help ensure that wasteful activities don't build up.

An Expectations Exchange

(FOR INDIVIDUALS OR WORK GROUPS)

This tool is a simple way of getting critical information out on the table. It often takes the threat away from candid conversations. A group approach is described in "Variation."

PREPARE

Identify the area of work in which you want to give and receive feedback. This could range from all aspects of work to feedback on a particular project. Make certain there is a solid business reason for the discussion.

Complete an expectations exchange sheet for the person (or group) you will meet with.

The other person does the same.

Here is the expectations exchange format:

I would like you to do more _____ because
_____.

I would like you to do less _____ because
_____.

I would like you to keep on doing _____
because _____.

PRESENT
One person reads his/her sheet.

LISTEN
The feedback recipient asks questions for clarification.

Repeat the process, with the recipient reading his/her expectations to the first person. Clarify.

ENGAGE IN DIALOGUE
Discuss points of agreement and disagreement.

PLAN FOR ACTION
Determine what actions each of you will take based on what you learned from the exchange.

Determine whether a follow-up meeting is needed.

ACKNOWLEDGE
Thank the person for taking part in the process.

VARIATION

Managers can use this process with staff who report directly to them. The manager completes an expectations exchange sheet for the staff as a group. The exchange might begin with, "I would like the staff to take more initiative in _____."

The staff meets to create a composite expectations exchange sheet for the manager.

Follow the process outlined in the six steps.

In using this variation, remember that people find it very difficult to give candid feedback to a boss. After all, you may have control over their performance review, assignments, and pay increases. Read "Guidelines for Receiving Feedback" in Part Three before using this variation.

PAY ATTENTION TO

Exchange is critical to this process. You must give—and receive—feedback.

Some managers hold expectations exchange meetings three or four times a year just to make sure the air remains clear.

PROJECT
DEBRIEFING

(FOR TEAMS)

Project teams need to examine how well they are functioning. Consider this a 10,000-mile checkup for your team. This conversation can come at the end of a project, or better yet, at key points throughout the project.

PREPARE
Consider the business reason for holding the meeting. Prepare a worksheet for everyone.

PRESENT
Ask everyone to *rate their satisfaction with the quality of the team's work*, using a scale from 1 to 7 (1 = poor, 7 = great). You should rate the team as well.

Ask each individual to state the grade he/she gave the group. Don't discuss the reasons for scores until everyone has given his/her score.

Ask each team member to explain the reasons for the grade he/she gave. Don't discuss or debate scores; simply listen.

LISTEN
Make sure people listen to each other. Resist the temptation to influence their opinions.

PRESENT AND LISTEN
Ask everyone to *identify how well the team is working together* using the 1 to 7 scale. You should rate the team as well.

Ask each individual to state the grade he/she gave the group.

Ask everyone to explain the reasons for the rating.

ENGAGE IN DIALOGUE
Discuss:

- What is working well on the team?

- What is hindering effectiveness?

Make sure the discussion takes into account the ratings on both quality and teamwork.

PLAN FOR ACTION
Identify actions the team can take to improve or maintain performance in the future.

ACKNOWLEDGE
Ask people what they thought of the process. Thank them for taking part.

PAY ATTENTION TO
Often when teams discuss work, they focus exclusively on the project and fail to address how they are working together. This exercise asks you to examine both aspects. How a team works together has a major impact on the quality of the work it does. The team may resist talking about itself, but it is worth pushing. During the first 10,000-mile checkup, conversation about the team may be superficial. That's fine. People are cautious. Next time they may say more.

This tool should not be an excuse to dump on people. Stick to the business reasons for debriefing.

If one person's scores are significantly different from those of other members on the team, the group may exert subtle pressure to get the wayward soul back in line. Resist the temptation to convert, since minority viewpoints provide valuable information. The way in which this person sees the world is true for him/her.

The leader should speak last. As one manager said, "Watch out for subtle domination by the team leader." People are likely to defer to you.

One manager told me, "I found better-quality feedback when the team leader's or facilitator's remarks were given last. I tried both ways, and feel that my comments influenced the group when I gave them early."

Be careful not to overreact. If people start blaming you for all the ills of the world, you may get defensive and say something you will later regret. Just listen and ask for clarification. This too shall pass.

Encourage everyone to speak. Facilitate the discussion to make sure it is truly a team debriefing and not just an opportunity for soapbox oratory from one person.

MANAGEMENT BY
WANDERING AROUND

(FOR INDIVIDUALS)

Peters and Waterman described *management by wandering around* (MBWA) in their seminal book, *In Search of Excellence*.[2] Unfortunately, *MBWA*, like *paradigm*, *empowerment*, and *TQM*, suffers from overuse. We tire of the term well before we understand the concept. Don't let that stop you from using it. MBWA works. It is informal, allows you to give and receive information, and makes you accessible to your staff.

PREPARE
Don't prepare. You shouldn't wander with a purpose. There is a difference between wandering and making a beeline. If each time you make your informal stroll you zing someone, it won't be long before people become wary of your presence.

PRESENT, LISTEN, ENGAGE IN DIALOGUE

Follow your interests and curiosity. Talk, listen, and engage as the spirit moves you. The less you plan, the more effective MBWA will be.

- Keep your eyes open. What's working? What isn't?

- Acknowledge good work.

- Make suggestions for fine-tuning if you can do so privately. If not, save the feedback for later.

- Ask questions.

- Get to know your staff.

PLAN FOR ACTION

As a result of the wandering, make notes about things you need to take action on. Perhaps you made a promise to someone or saw a quality problem needing attention.

ACKNOWLEDGE

Except for a simple "thank you" to people as you walk around, no other acknowledgment is necessary.

VARIATION

If your staff is housed in various locations, you may need to be creative. One manager uses electronic mail frequently and informally to stay in touch with his staff. Although face-to-face contact is best, use the means that are available.

PAY ATTENTION TO

Be careful not to jump over the chain of command and create other staff problems by interfering in people's work.

The first time you wander, people may not speak candidly.

One manager suggests, "MBWA becomes a habit. If you only walk around occasionally, it is inevitably a big deal and your associates will be uncomfortable. By making MBWA a part of your weekly schedule, your associates will relax, and you will see what is really happening, and your feedback will be used on the *real* process, not just the process that's followed when the boss is around."

I once suggested this tool to a client who was woefully out of touch with her staff. She replied, "I tried it once and it didn't work." Wandering only once won't do much good. People must get used to seeing you around.

POSITIVE FEEDBACK
FOR TEAMS

(TEAMS OR WORK GROUPS)

Most people receive precious little emotional support at work. Except for the occasional "thank you" and rubber chicken dinner, the workplace is often barren of significant positive feedback. This saps the spirit of most. People need to feel appreciated.

The following exercise is wonderful. I have seen people deeply moved by it. People may be reluctant, however, to take part in something that seems so "touchy-feely." If you work on a team that could use a dose of positive reinforcement, I encourage you to give it a try in spite of your reservations.

PREPARE

No preparation is needed, other than to make sure people are willing to take part.

PRESENT

Ask each member of the group to write his/her name on top of a blank sheet of paper and pass it to the left.

Each person writes one sentence about this person that begins, "I appreciate... ," "I admire...," or "I respect..." For example, one person may write, "I appreciate your willingness to stay until the job gets done."

The sheets are passed to the left once again, and each team member writes a sentence on the new sheet.

Continue this process until everyone has his/her own sheet back again. Each person should scan the comments received.

One person volunteers to pass his/her sheet around for oral comments. As it makes the rounds, each person reads the sentence he or she wrote and expands on it. For instance, "I wrote, 'I appreciate your willingness to stay until the job is done.' Often during the past few months you have stayed here well beyond closing time to make sure everything was ready to go out the next morning. That saved me a lot of headaches. Thanks."

Repeat the process so that everyone's written comments are read aloud.

LISTEN

During this process, the recipient of the feedback has a very simple job—shut up and listen. So often we talk away positive feedback—making excuses, giving credit to others, or telling the feedback givers why they are wrong.

ENGAGE IN DIALOGUE
No dialogue is needed.

PLAN FOR ACTION
No action is needed.

ACKNOWLEDGE
Hold a brief discussion. Ask people, "What did you think of this exercise?"

VARIATION
Post blank flip chart sheets around the room. Each person's name is written on a sheet. Individuals write comments randomly, using different colored markers. At the end of the exercise, the individual accepts and reads his/her sheet. This approach works well for a large team.

PAY ATTENTION TO
Don't force this tool on an unsuspecting group. Make sure people are willing to engage in it before you begin. That doesn't mean you shouldn't nudge them—simply don't inflict it on them.

Monitor the process. Make certain that recipients remain silent except to ask questions for clarification. The only declarative sentence allowed is "Thank you."

THE
PERFORMANCE
APPRAISAL

I hate performance appraisals. They work against the very thing we desire—improved performance. Peter Block, W. Edwards Deming, Philip Crosby, and Stephen Covey harangue against them, and if they can't change organizations' fascination with this annual bloodletting ritual, I don't imagine my words will help either. Nevertheless, I'll try.

Most performance review systems reinforce a paternalistic world, one built on distrust and the assumption that the boss knows more about our skills, abilities, and commitment than we do. This dependency works against empowerment. And focusing on individual performance problems, rather than looking at systems issues, works against the grain of quality improvement.

If you agree with this view and can influence your organization to change, go for it. Or if you can get around the system and avoid performance reviews, I wish you well. However, if you are a manager caught in the middle somewhere, with little power to change the system, at least consider the following ideas. They might help make your performance reviews a little more humane.

PREPARE

Do your homework. As Yogi Berra once said, "You've got to have deep depth." Do whatever it takes to find specific examples illustrating the points you want to make.

Support yourself. Consider how you will feel during the session. Determine ways to support yourself. Take time to review your notes prior to the meeting. Rehearse. Do something (short of guzzling cheap booze) so that you feel as relaxed and centered as possible going into the review. For example, you might take a short walk, sit quietly for a few moments, take a few deep breaths. And during the meeting, remember to breathe.

PRESENT

Stick to the point. Cato the Censor said, "Stick to the point and the words will take care of themselves." Prior to the meeting, decide what points you need to make. Be aware of what nervousness does to your own best intentions. Perhaps when adrenaline pumps, you find yourself overstating points—making global statements about the person and his/her work. Or perhaps you understate. In the heat of the moment, you back off and fail to say what needs to be said. Remember what you are there to accomplish.

Keep it simple and clear. There should be no surprises during a performance review. (If there are, apologize, and promise to do better in the future.) Make your point. Give an example or two.

Use customer information. Use data from your customers and other stakeholders as the basis for the review. These people are the reason you exist. Their comments should guide feedback. Also consider discussing those adaptive skills that have an impact on the work. (See "Preparing to Receive Feedback" in Part Three for a description of these skills.)

LISTEN
Shut up. Stop talking and make certain the recipient understands what you have said. You might ask him/her to paraphrase your comments.

Pace yourself. People can take in only so much before they are overwhelmed. Go slowly. Allow the recipient to respond, breathe, and ask questions. Out of nervousness, you may be inclined to rush the meeting simply to get the onerous event over with.

ENGAGE IN DIALOGUE

Build a partnership. Ask, "How can I assist you?" Find ways to help staff be successful. I don't mean that you do their job, but you might, for example, provide liaison to other units, coordinate work flow within the department, or work with suppliers to make sure resources get to your staff on time. This is an opportunity for you to receive feedback too.

Avoid grades. No one wants to get a B or a C. People translate number scales into letter grades. A students who fail to receive A's as a result of an arbitrary quota system will be furious. B and C students who receive these grades—even though accurate—will begin to live down to your expectations. I realize that many systems require you to give grades. Some sick review systems even set quotas for the number of top grades you are allowed to give. (So much for empowerment.) I encourage you to do what you can to get around the system and still keep your job.

Discuss the system. Since most performance problems are the result of a system flaw rather than a person's commitment, abilities, or skills, attention that is so focused on the individual seems misplaced. Discuss what needs to be changed to support this person in doing excellent work.

PLAN FOR ACTION

Focus on the future. The purpose of most performance appraisals is to improve performance—in the future. Get off past events as quickly as possible, and discuss ways you can work together better in the future.

ACKNOWLEDGE

Thank the other person for engaging in the discussion.

ACID BATH
FEEDBACK

Giving feedback can at times be difficult, even painful. The following suggestions, drawn from the "Performance Appraisal" section, can ease the process. Please review that section for a fuller explanation of each of the following steps.

PREPARE

Make certain you can give specific examples.

Rehearse.

Support yourself. Prepare thoroughly and breathe deeply and often.

PRESENT

Stick to the point. Keep your goal in mind. Don't be distracted by seductive side conversations. Going off on a tangent is simply a way for both of you to avoid the major issues.

Keep the feedback simple and clear. Go into the meeting prepared to talk about one or two points. Don't include everything you have ever wanted to say to this person.

Use critical information. Use customer and other stakeholder data as the basis for feedback.

LISTEN

Go slowly. Think of an old steam boiler with its pressure-release valve. When things begin to heat up, you both need to be able to cool down. Allow silence. Time to breathe. Time for the other person to respond. Consider taking a break.

ENGAGE IN DIALOGUE

Build a partnership. Discuss your own role in improving performance in the future. Take responsibility for your part of the problem. If you don't see yourself as part of the problem, think again before inflicting your thoughts on the other person. Problems are seldom one-sided.

PLAN FOR ACTION

The past is gone, and you want things to improve in the future. Remember, it is hard to be defensive about the future, since it hasn't happened yet.

PART THREE

TOOLS FOR

RECEIVING FEEDBACK

"TO INFLUENCE, WE MUST BE WILLING TO BE INFLUENCED."

— ANONYMOUS

PREPARING TO RECEIVE FEEDBACK

Throughout this toolkit, I have urged you to ask for feedback that is job related. Although using these tools will get at important issues, you may not hear important feedback about your own work. If, for instance, your approach to working with staff rivals Genghis Khan's, people will be reluctant to speak candidly. And the feedback you do receive will never address the underlying problem. Consequently, you will get a false sense of what is real.

The Leadership Institute of Seattle (LIOS) and Richard Bolles developed a model that speaks to this dilemma.[3] The skills we need at work are divided into three major categories:

- *Work content skills.* These are the specific skills needed to perform a particular job. For an engineer, as an example, they are all the skills that go with engineering. When good feedback is given at work, it usually relates to work content skills, since others are most comfortable talking about an area where measurement is so clear.

- *Functional skills.* These skills, which are more transferable from job to job, include the ability to run a meeting, lead a project team, make a briefing, give speeches, and so forth. Often we receive little feedback in this area. This handbook may help you address many of the functional skills you need.

- *Adaptive skills.* These are basic "getting along with people" skills. As former LIOS associate John Runyon once said, "They are things we hope our children learn, but no one ever teaches."

Adaptive skills can help you perform the other skill sets effectively. Neglect or misuse of these skills can seriously impede your performance—and can even threaten your career.

Here are some adaptive skills that I believe are important for managers.

Straightforwardness. During the height of the Reagan era, Barry Goldwater, the patriarch of American conservatives in this country, said he believed that the best president of the past 100 years was the liberal Democrat Harry S Truman. He said, "I never went to bed at night wondering where Harry stood on anything." With straightforward people, *what you see is what you get.*[4]

Keeping things in perspective. People with a big-picture viewpoint are able to take their work seriously, while not taking themselves too seriously. They are the calm within the storm. We all know people whose sole contribution to a raging fire is to bring gasoline, while others seem to handle every crisis confidently and calmly.

In the 1983 World Series, Phillie short-reliever Tug McGraw pitched brilliantly in late-inning situations. But as he left the field his pitching arm would tremble wildly. Reporters asked how he could pitch so well when he seemed so nervous. He said that when he began to get tense on the mound, he would say to himself, "Someday, when our sun goes supernova and the world turns to a ball of ice, what difference will this pitch have made?" Then he pitched the ball.

Keeping commitments. With these people, their word is their bond. If they say they will have a draft to you by Friday at 4:00, you know it will be on your desk by that time.

Awareness of impact on others. Some people, while far from perfect, know the impact they have on others. This quality allows them to hold their weaknesses in check and take corrective action when they blow it. Joe Bltsplk, a pathetic creature in Al Capp's "L'il Abner" comic strip, personified the antithesis of this skill. Wherever he appeared, trains collided, businesses went belly-up, robberies increased. Joe meandered through life, oblivious to the fact that his presence caused these disasters. Organizations are filled with Joe's cousins. To avoid being one, take a look at your responses as if you were in the other person's shoes.

Sensitivity to people. Some managers work as if they believe in the Golden Rule, treating others with dignity and respect. Although other "textbook managers" seem to do all the right things, their style and manner with others is abrasive. Their praise is hollow. Their disdain for others is apparent. Be sincere—you and your colleagues will know the difference.

Ability to self-correct. In my study of effective middle management practices, I found that the best managers were not perfect human beings, but they did have the capacity to learn from their mistakes.

This list of adaptive skills is not definitive. I urge you to create your own list. Look around you. What are the things people say behind others' backs? As you look at poor Bernie drooling in the corner, consider the reasons why his career stalled years ago. Why do people like working with Sally, and why does she excel where others fail? This informal assessment will help you begin to see which adaptive skills are critical for success in your organization.

Asking for feedback on your own adaptive skills is difficult. Most aren't comfortable talking about such *personal* issues, yet these skills are essential. Since others are likely to avoid telling you what everyone already knows, getting feedback can be tricky. The guidelines listed on the following pages are particularly important with regard to these skills.

GUIDELINES FOR
RECEIVING FEEDBACK

Determine if you want to hear feedback on work content, functional, or adaptive skills. Use the following guidelines in combination with the specific tools that follow to make sure you receive the best possible feedback from these encounters.

Place clear boundaries around the feedback. Let people know what you want and how much feedback you are prepared to hear today. If you fail to define precisely what you want and who you want to hear from, you run the risk of hearing too much. Once that happens, you may get defensive. You may shut down and close the others out or you may lash out at those who are trying to tell the truth as they see it. In either case, it will be far more difficult for people to be candid in the future.

Listen beneath the words. Listen for subtle cues embedded in the feedback you receive on work content and functional skills. You may hear a phrase—or something in a person's voice—that indicates a potential adaptive skill problem.

Explore gently. You might ask, "Is there anything in my style that is getting in the way of our meeting this goal?" You may receive no feedback or you may hear a polite comment that begins to touch on an adaptive skill. Be grateful and consider what the person said.

Don't defend yourself. If you want feedback, you must accept that what others tell you is true from their vantage point. You don't have to believe it. You aren't obligated to do anything differently as a result of hearing it, but you must listen openly. At the first sign that you are defending your actions, others may stop telling you their truth.

Express your thanks. Let people know you appreciate their candor. After you have had time to think about the feedback, tell them ways in which the feedback was helpful.

DON'T
FORGET SARA

Feedback can be overwhelming. When this happens, you are likely to experience its impact in stages. Understanding this natural progression of reactions may help you deal with the news more calmly—and keep you from taking some action you may regret. So, when you receive feedback, think of SARA.

SARA stands for Surprise, Anger, Rationalization, and Acceptance.

SURPRISE

When you first hear feedback, you may be surprised or shocked. You may not be sure how to respond. This reaction is natural and healthy. You are simply protecting yourself from taking in too much too quickly. Honor this response.

When you are in S, the best action is no action. Allow yourself time to be in here. Don't try to make decisions or plans—simply trust that this feeling will pass.

ANGER

Surprise is replaced by anger. "How can they do this to me?" If the feedback came anonymously, you may wonder, "Who said what?" Once again, anger is natural and will pass. Enjoy the ride.

Don't take any action while you are feeling angry. You will only do damage.

RATIONALIZATION

During rationalization, you are likely to make reasonable excuses. Your statements sound as if you are back in control. You may sound logical and all together, but you aren't.

During this phase you may try to make sense of the feedback by making excuses. "Well, I wasn't surprised they rated me low on planning. After all, they've only known me for seven years. Once they get to know my work..."

ACCEPTANCE

You can now look at the feedback with some degree of objectivity, take what is useful, and disregard the rest. You can digest what you've heard and determine what provides nourishment and what should be eliminated.

We cannot rush SARA, she moves at her own pace. When feedback is overwhelming or particularly surprising we may find ourselves remaining in Surprise and Anger for a long time. At other times, we may feel ourselves moving through the stages quickly.

FEEDBACK
FROM STAFF

The higher you are in the organization, the more difficult it is to get candid feedback about your own performance. Most performance appraisal processes don't allow for upward feedback. You must ask for it.

People learn at a very early age to not criticize parents, teachers, or bosses. This reluctance is hardwired into us. If you want people to go against their nature, you must ask for feedback again and again and again. The first time you ask for feedback, your staff may be skeptical. They may speculate that you just read a new book on how to give and receive feedback, and they may decide to lie low for a few days until you forget all about this nonsense.

If you receive any feedback at all, it may be only superficial. Take delight in what you get, and the next time you may get a little more. Giving feedback to one's supervisor is like deciding to swim in a strange pond. People want to test the waters. They put in a toe, and if that doesn't feel too bad, they put an entire foot in the water and so on until they feel comfortable swimming freely. Allow people to dabble their toes in the water for awhile.

PREPARE

Consider what you need feedback on. Make sure there is a solid business reason for getting feedback. Perhaps it will help you improve efficiency, conduct meetings, coordinate work among departments, or lead projects.

Consider this question: From your staff's point of view, what potential benefit might they see from giving you feedback?

Limit the request for feedback to one or two items. (You want to make this easy for them. If you ask for too much, you will overwhelm them and possibly yourself.)

Determine who you want to hear from. Perhaps you can get what you need from one person, from a series of one-to-one meetings, or from the entire group en masse. (If the thought of hearing feedback from a large group makes your stomach turn, trust that biological response, and limit feedback to one-on-one meetings.)

PRESENT

Explain what you would like feedback on—and explain why the feedback is important to you.

If people are reluctant to speak, you might prime the pump by giving an example. "It seems to me that the way I jump from topic to topic in staff meetings might be confusing to you. Is that a problem? Would I do better to stick to a one-topic-at-a-time agenda?"

LISTEN

Listen to the responses. Ask questions to make sure you understand what they are saying. Don't defend yourself, make excuses, or blame someone else.

ENGAGE IN DIALOGUE

If the message you hear is heavy, don't engage in a dialogue. You need time to consider what you've just heard. If you speak now, you may make promises you will regret later. Or worse, you may react defensively and lash out at the other person.

PLAN FOR ACTION

Summarize what you have heard.

If appropriate, tell them what you plan to do with the feedback.

ACKNOWLEDGE

Thank them for their help.

VARIATION

Management in an office in one company routinely

meets with nonmanagement staff to ask, "What are we doing that bugs you?" During these meetings, people often identify the hassles that inhibit effective work.

PAY ATTENTION TO

One manager said, "I find it best to be specific on what I want feedback on by providing a recent example. Otherwise the staff member is reluctant to dive in. Sticking to the specific incident seems to take the personal attack out of it, and makes it easier for me to listen." Another manager suggests, "Bosses need to model receiving feedback, even if they do it inelegantly."

FEEDBACK
FROM YOUR BOSS

Not knowing where you stand with your boss can be a career killer. If you care about your career, you must manage this relationship as well.

PREPARE
Consider this question: What is the potential benefit to your boss for giving you feedback?

Make sure there is a solid business reason for engaging him or her in this discussion.

Think about the one or two specific items you need feedback on in order to do your job brilliantly.

PRESENT
State what you want clearly and specifically. Explain why this feedback is important.

LISTEN

Listen to his/her responses. Ask questions to make sure you understand what you are being told. Don't defend yourself.

ENGAGE IN DIALOGUE

If your boss delivers a heavy blow, don't engage in a dialogue. You need time to consider what you've just heard. If you speak now you may over-promise. Give yourself time to chew on the information.

PLAN FOR ACTION

Summarize what you have heard.

If you are ready, tell the boss what you plan to do based on what you learned today. If not, explain that you will think over what you heard and get back to him or her soon. Make sure you do so.

ACKNOWLEDGE

Thank him/her for the help.

PAY ATTENTION TO

Most often you should have solid business reasons for having such a discussion with your boss. But let's say you are feeling insecure or uncertain about your position, and you would like to hear what your boss has to say. Unfortunately, that insecurity may make it difficult for you to engage in a highly personal exchange—a real Catch-22.

Beginning with a *solid business discussion* may make it easier to engage in a more difficult personal discussion at some later time. Or perhaps this business discussion may even begin to answer some of the unasked questions. For instance, your boss might say, "Well, Sylvia, I wouldn't worry about the Inco account. You probably won't be around long enough for it to matter much." And there you have your answer. Even though you may not like what you hear, at least now you can make decisions based on facts, not perceptions.

FEEDBACK
FROM PEERS

Increasingly, people find that they must rely heavily on peers or colleagues in other departments. Often no one reports officially to anyone else in these peer relationships, and therefore feedback is nonexistent. It is in your best interests to keep these relationships open and clean. Your peers are your suppliers and your customers. Without good communication with suppliers, you may suffer delays and other problems. If internal customers are unhappy, you are not doing your job. Finally, peers talk. People are picked for plum assignments and considered for promotions based on informal grapevine assessments. You need to know what your peers are thinking and saying about you.

PREPARE

Your peers fall into one of three camps:

- *Suppliers.* These individuals or groups represent work units that supply you and your office with information, support, or resources.

- *Customers.* These individuals or groups are major recipients of your products or services.

- *Project or task force.* These people work with you on a team that examines some business issue.

Determine where each person or group fits. The questions you ask will be determined by your relationship.

Prepare specific questions for the meeting.

- Ask suppliers what they need from you to do their job most effectively. Even though you are the customer, you may be doing things that prevent your suppliers from giving you the best service.

- Ask customers what they like about your product or service, what they dislike, and what they would like to see changed.

- Ask project or task force members what you could be doing to serve the team more effectively. Consider using the team "10,000-mile checkup" with this group (see "Project Debriefing" in Part Two).

PRESENT

Explain what you would like feedback on and why it is important to you, as well as the potential benefit to them.

Ask the questions you prepared.

LISTEN

Listen to their responses. Ask questions to make sure you understand what they are saying.

ENGAGE IN DIALOGUE

This may be an opportunity to engage in an informal expectations exchange with your peers. Since you led the way, others may now be willing to discuss ways in which you can assist each other in the future. Don't force this to happen. Pursue this course only if others initiate it.

PLAN FOR ACTION

Summarize what you heard.

If appropriate, tell them what you plan to do with the feedback.

ACKNOWLEDGE
Thank them for their help.

VARIATION
The Expectations Exchange works well in peer relationships (read about that tool in Part Two). Of course, you must get others to buy in before proceeding.

FEEDBACK
FROM A COACH

Often I recommend to clients who are trying to improve their job performance that they pick a coach or mentor to assist them.

The coach should be:

- someone you trust and will listen to

- someone who has frequent opportunities to see you in action

- someone who has nothing to gain or lose from engaging in these conversations. The coach should not be someone who reports to you.

PREPARE

Determine the areas in which you would like to receive coaching.

Identify someone who meets the criteria listed above, and see if he/she would be willing to work with you.

Pick a regular time to meet and discuss your progress. For example, you might meet for lunch once a month.

PRESENT

Remind him/her of what you are looking for.

During this meeting you might ask for feedback on a particular issue, or for help in meeting a future challenge. Or you might debrief an incident that didn't go as you had planned.

LISTEN

Listen to what your coach has to say. Listen deeply. Try to understand what he/she is telling you.

It is OK to defend yourself when meeting with your coach. However, once you have given the rationale as to why your actions were perfect, listen to what your coach has to say. Does he/she agree with your assessment?

ENGAGE IN DIALOGUE AND PLAN FOR

ACTION

Together, brainstorm actions you might take in the future.

ACKNOWLEDGE
Thank him/her for the continued help.

VARIATION
Although I work alone much of the time, I call on col-leagues to coach me from afar. I explain the situation that has occurred, and once they stop laughing, I get their reactions and advice. I find it extremely helpful. So, even if the person who can be most helpful to you lives hundreds of miles away, you can still engage in productive exchanges over the phone.

FEEDBACK
FROM QUESTIONNAIRES

You may have an opportunity to receive feedback through a formal questionnaire from your boss, peers, and staff. This information can be invaluable, but you must be ready to receive it.[5]

Many training and development companies offer survey questionnaires that assess management performance on issues such as planning, motivation, and technical knowledge. They can be eye-opening and quite helpful. Often this process is referred to as "360° feedback" in that you receive feedback from all around—boss, peers, and staff.

SELECTING A QUESTIONNAIRE
The following items may help you choose the appropriate questionnaire for your purposes.

Examine the items on the questionnaire. Will this it measure the management practices on which you need feedback? If a questionnaire focuses primarily on performance in face-to-face meetings and you work with your staff over modems and phones, you may need to search for a better instrument.

Be wary of questionnaires that simply use adjectives such as "forceful," "directive," and "supportive." Adjectives are subject to too many varied interpretations. You may end up feeling bad without the benefit of learning what you could do differently. What possible good can it do to learn that 20 percent of your staff feel you are "adaptable" *and* that they don't like it? What does "adaptable" mean? What should you change? Look for items that delineate precisely what you are doing right and wrong.

Determine how many people will fill it out. The federal government offers managers a well-written but poorly executed feedback tool that gives the manager a comparative score showing your own evaluation as well as what the boss has to say. Getting feedback from one person is far too limited. What if that person happens to be a jerk? Look for a questionnaire that allows you to give it to multiple bosses, staff reporting to you, and peers.

Get help in interpreting the results. Survey feedback can be overwhelming. Make sure that the vendor or someone within your organization is skilled at interpreting the results of this particular tool. Don't go it alone. 360° feedback can be extremely powerful. You need to be assured that someone will walk you through the results.

USING THE QUESTIONNAIRE
Consider the following once you decide to use a 360° questionnaire.

Choose people wisely. If you have the opportunity to choose who fills out the questionnaire, make sure you pick people who know you, people you respect, and people who will give you a candid assessment. The more care you take in selecting people, the higher the quality of feedback you will receive.

Determine what you want. Before you look at the results, identify what you want to learn. Are you are interested in learning more about your leadership style? How well you keep people informed? How others view your project-planning skills?

If you know the categories on the questionnaire, determine which areas are highest priority for your work before looking at the results.

360° feedback can be overwhelming (remember SARA). If you go into the process knowing what you need, you are less likely to get lost in a mass of data or psychobabble.

Eat slowly and chew your food. Some 360° feedback instruments are long and cover many areas of management. Take your time with this feast. Read it. Walk away. Come back, read some more. A few days later, look at the results again. Allow yourself time to take in the information. You can't eat the entire meal in a single sitting.

Look for similarities among groups. Notice patterns among the responses. Is everyone saying you are great at planning and need to work on your writing skills? Focus on these common themes.

Look for differences among groups. Be interested in why your boss rates you high in an area while your staff rates you low.

Thank those who responded. Too often, feedback falls into a black hole. The respondents never know your reactions. At the very least, you owe them a "thank you." Ideally, you will use the results to engage in further conversations.

Consider this a first step. Even the best questionnaires raise more questions. For example, the results may make you curious about why your peers see your project management skills so differently than you do.

Use other tools in this handbook to help you enrich this feedback. The tools for receiving feedback from a coach, from staff, and from peers may be especially helpful.

"I WANT PEOPLE TO TELL ME THE TRUTH, EVEN IF IT COSTS THEM THEIR JOBS."

— SAMUEL GOLDWYN

NOTES

1. Mark Frohman and Perry Pascarella, "American Management Operates in the Dark: *Industry Week Magazine Survey," Industry Week*, May 20, 1991, 25–29

2. Tom Peters and Robert Waterman, *In Search of Excellence: Lessons from America's Best-Run Companies*, New York: Harper and Row, 1982.

3. John Scherer, "Job Related Adaptive Skills: Toward Personal Growth," in *1980 Annual Handbook for Group Facilitators*, La Jolla, Calif.: University Associates.

4. Barry Goldwater, *Goldwater*, New York: Doubleday, 1988.

5. Some of the text is adapted with permission from Rick Maurer, *Caught in the Middle: A Leadership Guide for Partnership in the Workplace*, Portland, Ore.: Productivity Press, 1992, Chapter 17.

ABOUT THE AUTHOR

Rick Maurer is the author of *Caught in the Middle: A Leadership Guide for Partnership in the Workplace* (Productivity Press, 1992), as well as several articles on management and employee empowerment in publications such as *Excellence*, *Quality Observer*, and *Total Quality Management*. Since 1978 he has worked with clients through his consulting practice, Maurer & Associates. Most of his work focuses on helping clients find ways to include people in the planning and implementation of organizational change. In the interest of stimulating feedback, the author invites readers to contact him at:

Rick Maurer
Maurer & Associates
703-525-7074 (telephone)
703-525-0183 (fax)
470-9929@MCIMAIL.COM (internet)

BOOKS FROM PRODUCTIVITY PRESS

Productivity Press publishes and distributes materials on continuous improvement in productivity, quality, and the creative involvement of all employees. Supplemental products and services include membership groups, conferences, seminars, in-house training and consulting, audio-visual training programs, and industrial study missions. Call toll-free 1-800-394-6868 for our free catalog.

Caught in the Middle
A Leadership Guide for Partnership in the Workplace
Rick Maurer

Managers today are caught between old skills and new expectations. You're expected not only to improve quality and services, but also to get staff more involved. This stimulating book provides the inspiration and know-how to achieve these goals as it brings to light the rewards of establishing a real partnership with your staff. Includes self-assessment questionnaires.
ISBN 1-56327-004-8 / 258 pages / $29.95 / Order CAUGHT-B232

PRODUCTIVITY PRESS, INC., DEPT. BK, P.O. BOX 13390, PORTLAND, OR 97213-0390
Telephone: 1-800-394-6868   Fax: 1-800-394-6286